Julius Caesar

William Shakespeare

Julius Caesar

William Shakespeare

Abridged and adapted by Emily Hutchinson

Illustrated by Steve Moore

A PACEMAKER CLASSIC

GLOBE FEARON

Pearson Learning Group

Executive Editor: Joan Carrafiello
Project Editor: Karen Bernhaut
Editorial Assistant: Keisha Carter
Production Director: Penny Gibson
Print Buyer: Cheryl Johnson
Production Editor: Alan Dalgleish
Desktop Specialist: Margarita T. Linnartz
Art Direction: Joan Jacobus
Marketing Manager: Marge Curson
Cover and Interior Illustrations: Steve Moore
Cover Design: Margarita T. Linnartz

ISBN 0-8359-1238-8

Printed in the United States of America

7 8 9 10   06 05 04 03

Globe
Fearon

Pearson Learning Group

1-800-321-3106
www.pearsonlearning.com

Contents

Cast of Characters

JULIUS CAESAR	Leader of the Roman Empire
OCTAVIUS, ANTONY, AND LEPIDUS	Leaders after the death of Caesar
CICERO, PUBLIUS, AND POPILIUS	Senators of Rome
BRUTUS, CASSIUS, CASCA, TREBONIUS, LIGARIUS, DECIUS, METELLUS, AND CINNA	Plotters against Caesar
FLAVIUS AND MURELLUS	Law officers
ARTEMIDORUS	A teacher
SOOTHSAYER	A teller of the future
LUCILIUS, TITINIUS, MESSALA, AND YOUNG CATO	Friends of Brutus and Cassius
LUCIUS AND STRATO	Servants of Brutus
PINDARUS	Servant of Cassius
CALPURNIA	Wife of Caesar
PORTIA	Wife of Brutus

Act 1

Caesar returns to Rome in victory, and the working people have a day off to celebrate. Flavius and Murellus, seeing Caesar as a threat to Rome's Republican rule, stop the celebration. A soothsayer, or prophet, warns Caesar to be careful, but Caesar does not take the warning seriously. Behind Caesar's back, some men whom he considers friends plan to kill him. They want to get Brutus in on the plot.

Scene 1

A street in Rome. FLAVIUS, MURELLUS, *and some* COMMONERS *enter.*

FLAVIUS: Get off the streets,
　　You lazy creatures!
　　Go home! Is this a holiday?
　　Don't you know that you should not
　　Be walking around on a workday
　　Without the tools of your trade? Tell me,
　　What is your trade?

COMMONER: I am a cobbler, sir.
　　It is a trade that I use in good conscience.
　　Indeed, sir, I am a mender of bad soles.
　　All that I live by is with the awl.
　　You see, I use my awl to mend old shoes.
　　I am, in a way, sir, a doctor to old shoes.
　　When they are in great danger,
　　I recover them.

FLAVIUS: Why are you not in your shop?
　　Why are you in the streets today?

1

COMMONER: Well, sir, if I lead these men
About the streets, their shoes will wear out.
Then I can get myself some more work.
But I am just joking, sir. The truth is that
We are having a holiday, to see Caesar
And to celebrate his victory.

MURELLUS : Why are you celebrating?
What victory has he won?
What captives are following him to Rome?
You blocks, you stones,
You worse-than-senseless things!
Oh, you hard hearts,
You cruel men of Rome!
Did you not know Pompey?
Have you not climbed up the city walls,
To towers and windows, even to rooftops,
With your babies in your arms? Did you not
Sit there all day, waiting to see Pompey
Pass through the streets of Rome?
And when you saw him,
Did you not cheer and shout?
And do you now put on your best clothes?
And do you now declare a holiday?
And do you now lay flowers in the path
Of the man who comes in victory
Over Pompey's blood? Be gone!
Run to your houses, fall on your knees,
Pray to the gods to stop the plague
That they must send to punish you!

FLAVIUS: Go, go, good countrymen.
Call a meeting of all poor men like you.

Meet on the banks of the Tiber River,
And weep your tears into the river.
(COMMONERS *exit.*)
See, Murellus, how they leave in silence.
They must feel guilty for what they do.
You go that way, toward the Capitol.
I will go this way. If you see any banners
Honoring Caesar, pull them down.

MURELLUS : Do you think we should?

FLAVIUS: Of course! The more feathers
We pluck from Caesar's wings, the lower
He will fly. Otherwise, he'll soar
Above us all and keep us in fear.

(*All exit.*)

Scene 2

A public place. CAESAR, ANTONY, CALPURNIA,
PORTIA, DECIUS, CICERO, BRUTUS, CASSIUS, CASCA, *a*
SOOTHSAYER, MURELLUS , *and* FLAVIUS *enter.*

CAESAR: Calpurnia!

CALPURNIA: Here, my lord.

CAESAR: Stand in Antony's path
During the sacred race on this feast day.
If he touches you as he runs, perhaps
You will be able to have a child for us.
It is said that childless women, if touched
In this race, can soon bear children.
And Antony!

ANTONY: Caesar, my lord?

CAESAR: Forget not, in your speed,
To touch Calpurnia. We want a child.

ANTONY: I shall remember, my lord.

SOOTHSAYER: Caesar!

CAESAR: Who calls?

SOOTHSAYER: Beware the ides of March.

CAESAR: Who said that?

BRUTUS: A soothsayer warned you
To take care on March 15th.

CAESAR: Let me see his face.

CASCA: Fellow, come from the crowd.
Look upon Caesar.

CAESAR: What did you say?

SOOTHSAYER: Beware the ides of March.

CAESAR: He is a dreamer. Let us leave him.

(*Trumpets sound.* ALL *but* BRUTUS *and* CASSIUS *exit.*)

CASSIUS: Will you watch the runners?

BRUTUS: No, not I.

CASSIUS: Please do.

BRUTUS: I am not interested in the race.
I lack that quick spirit that is in Antony.
But let me not stand in your way, Cassius.
I'll leave you.

CASSIUS: Brutus, I've noticed that
You seem different lately. You are distant.

It seems as if you no longer care for the
Friends that love you.

BRUTUS: Cassius, do not take it personally.
If I seem distant, it is because I am troubled
With confusing thoughts
Of concern only to myself.
I don't want any of my friends—
Such as you, Cassius—to think that I have
Forgotten about them.

CASSIUS: Then I have misjudged you.
Tell me, Brutus, can you see your face?

BRUTUS: Of course not.
The eye cannot see itself. It can only see
Its reflection.

CASSIUS: You are right, Brutus.
And it is too bad that there are no mirrors
To show you your own hidden value.

BRUTUS: Cassius, I think it is dangerous to
Seek in myself things that are not there.

CASSIUS: That is why, good Brutus,
I will act as your mirror. I will show you
Things in yourself
That you do not yet know about.

(*Noise and shouting are heard.*)

BRUTUS: Listen to that shouting!
I do fear that the people
Choose Caesar for their king.

CASSIUS: Ah, do you fear it?
That makes me think you do not want it.

BRUTUS: No, I don't Cassius.
Yet I love him well.
But why do you hold me here so long?
What is it that you wanted to talk about?

CASSIUS: Honor is the subject of my story.
I was born as free as Caesar. So were you.
We both have eaten as well as he.
We can both endure the winter's cold
As well as he. Once, on a cold, windy day,
I stood with Caesar on the banks
Of the Tiber River. Caesar said to me,
"Do you dare, Cassius, to leap with me
Into this angry river,
And swim to the other side?"
As soon as he said it, I jumped in
Dressed as I was and dared him to follow.
So indeed he did. The river roared,
And we swam as hard as we could.
But before we got to the shore,
Caesar cried, "Help me, Cassius,
       or I'll sink!"
I carried the tired Caesar from the
Waves of the Tiber. Now this man
Has become like a god. I am just
A wretched creature who must do as
he says. And when he was sick in Spain,
I noticed how he shook with fever.
I heard him groan.
That tongue of his, which gave such
Fine speeches, cried out,
"Give me some drink," like a sick child.

It amazes me that a man of such weakness
Could rise to such glory.

(*Noise and shouting are heard.*)

BRUTUS: Another loud shout!
I believe that the noise is for
Some new honors that are given to Caesar.

CASSIUS: Why, he stands over the
Narrow world like a huge statue while
We small men walk under his huge legs.
We try to find ourselves humble graves.
Men at some time are masters of their fates.
The fault, dear Brutus, is not in our stars.
It is in ourselves.
That is why we are underlings.
Why should his name be more important
Than yours?
Write them together: Brutus and Caesar.
Yours is as good a name as his.
Say them out loud.
Yours sounds just as good.
Weigh them. Yours is just as heavy.
Now, in the names of the gods,
Upon what meat does our Caesar feed
That causes him to grow so great?

BRUTUS: I have asked the same questions.
I have thought of this and of these times.
I will think about what you said.
Let us meet at a later time to talk about it.
Till then, my noble friend, remember this:
Brutus would rather live in a small village

Than call himself a son of Rome now.
I am afraid of what might happen to Rome,
If Caesar becomes king.

CASSIUS: I am glad that my weak words
Have struck this much fire from Brutus.

(CAESAR *and his followers enter again.*)

BRUTUS: The games are done, and
Caesar is returning.

CASSIUS: As they pass by,
Pull Casca by his sleeve.
He can tell us what happened.

BRUTUS: I will do so. But look, Cassius,
Caesar appears to be angry.
And all the rest look upset.
Calpurnia's cheek is pale, and Cicero
Seems to be disturbed about something.

CASSIUS: Casca will tell us what's wrong.

CAESAR: Antony!

ANTONY: Caesar?

CAESAR: Let the men who surround me
Be fat, healthy, and able to sleep at night.
That Cassius has a lean and hungry look.
He thinks too much.
Such men are dangerous.

ANTONY: Fear him not, Caesar.
He is not dangerous.
He is a noble Roman and a loyal one.

CAESAR: If only he were fatter!

But I am not afraid of him.
Yet if I were to be afraid of anyone,
It would be that thin Cassius.
He reads so much. He is a great observer.
He looks right through the deeds of men.
He doesn't enjoy plays, as you do, Antony.
He hears no music. He seldom smiles.
And when he does, it looks as if he mocks
His own spirit for smiling at anything.
Such men as he are never at ease when
They see someone greater than them-
selves.
And therefore, they are very dangerous.
I am only telling you what is to be feared—
Not what I fear—for always I am Caesar.
Stand on my right, for my left ear is deaf.
Tell me truly what you think of him.

(CAESAR *and followers exit, except* CASCA.)

CASCA: You pulled my sleeve.
Did you want to speak with me?

BRUTUS: Yes, Casca. What happened?
Why does Caesar look so sad?

CASCA: Weren't you out there?

BRUTUS: If I had been out there,
I wouldn't be asking you what happened.

CASCA: Well, a crown was offered to him.
But he pushed it away
With the back of his hand.
Then the people started to shout.

BRUTUS: What was the second shout for?

CASCA: Why, for the very same thing.

CASSIUS: They shouted three times.
　　What was the third shout for?

CASCA: Why, for the same thing again.

BRUTUS: The crown was offered three times?

CASCA: Yes, indeed, it was.
　　He pushed the crown away three times,
　　Each time more softly than before.
　　Every time he did so, the people shouted.

CASSIUS: Who offered him the crown?

CASCA: Antony did.

BRUTUS: Tell us how, gentle Casca.

CASCA: Mark Antony held out a crown—
　　It was one of those grand coronets.
　　And, as I told you, Caesar pushed it away.
　　But it looked as if he really wanted it.
　　Then Antony offered it to him again.
　　Once again, Caesar pushed it away,
　　But I could tell that he didn't want to.
　　Then Antony offered it a third time.
　　Again, Caesar pushed it away.
　　As he did so, the crowd hooted and
　　Clapped and tossed their hats into the air.
　　They gave out stinking breath.
　　It almost choked Caesar, for he swooned
　　And fell down. I could hardly keep from
　　Laughing, but I controlled myself.
　　If I had opened my mouth to laugh,
　　I would have had to breathe that foul air.

CASSIUS: Caesar swooned?

CASCA: Yes, he fell down, and was speechless.

BRUTUS: It's very likely.
He has the falling sickness.
But what did he say when he came to?

CASCA: Well, before he swooned,
He could see that the crowd was glad
That he had refused the crown.
He motioned to me to open his shirt.
Then he offered the crowd his throat to cut.
After that, he fainted. When he came to,
He said that if he had done anything wrong,
It was because of his sickness.
Several women standing near me cried,
"What a good man!"
They forgave him with all their hearts.
But we can't pay attention to them.
If Caesar had stabbed their mothers,
They would have acted the same way.

BRUTUS: And after that, did he seem sad?

CASCA: Yes.

CASSIUS: Did Cicero say anything?

CASCA: Yes, he spoke in Greek, but
I couldn't understand a word of it.
You could say that it was Greek to me.
And here's some more news:
Murellus and Flavius have been
Fired from their jobs for pulling down

All decorations of Caesar's image.
But, farewell. I must go now.

CASSIUS: Let's have dinner tonight.

CASCA: No, I already have plans.

CASSIUS: What about tomorrow night?

CASCA: Yes, if I am alive, and you are well,
And the dinner is worth eating.

CASSIUS: Good. I will expect you.

CASCA: See you then. Good-bye for now.

(CASCA *exits.*)

BRUTUS: I must go, too, Cassius.
Tomorrow, let's get together to talk.

CASSIUS: Till then, think of the world.
(BRUTUS *exits.*)
Well, Brutus, you are noble. Yet, I see
That your noble nature may be changed
By the company it keeps. Therefore,
It is best for noble minds to keep company
Only with others like themselves.
For who is so strong
That he cannot be changed?
Tonight, I will write notes in several
Different handwritings. Then I'll put them
Where Brutus will see them. He'll think
They came from several people. Each one
Will say that the people of Rome love him.
They will also say how dangerous Caesar is.

After this, let Caesar watch his ways.
For we will stop him, or suffer worse days.

(CASSIUS *exits*.)

Scene 3

A street. Thunder and lightning. CICERO *and* CASCA, *with his sword drawn, enter.*

CICERO: Good evening, Casca.
What's wrong?
Why do you look so worried?

CASCA: Doesn't it worry you when
The whole earth seems to shake
Like this? Oh, Cicero, I have seen
Storms when the scolding winds
Have torn apart the strong oaks.
I have seen the ocean swell and rage
And foam to be one with the clouds.
But never till tonight, never till now,
Have I seen a storm dropping fire.
Either there is a war in heaven,
Or else the world has offended the gods,
And the gods have sent this destruction.

CICERO: Tell me what you saw.

CASCA: A commoner—you know him—
Held up his left hand. It flamed and burned
Like 20 torches joined.
Yet his hand was not scorched.
Not only that—I still have my sword out—
Near the Capitol, I met a lion.
He stared at me and went proudly by

Without harming me. And I met a group
Of 100 frightened women.
They swore they saw men in flames
Walking up and down the streets.
And yesterday, the owl, that bird of night,
Sat in the plaza at noon,
Hooting and shrieking.
When such things happen,
I believe that they are omens
About what might happen in Rome.

CICERO: Indeed, you tell of strange things.
But they might not mean what you think.
Will Caesar come to the Capitol tomorrow?

CASCA: Yes, he will.
He told Antony to tell you so.

CICERO: Good night, then, Casca.
This disturbed sky is not to walk in.

CASCA: Farewell, Cicero.

(CICERO *exits.* CASSIUS *enters.*)

CASSIUS: Who's there?

CASCA: A Roman.

CASSIUS: You sound like Casca.

CASCA: Your ear is good, Cassius.
What a night this is!

CASSIUS: A very pleasing night
To honest men.

CASCA: Who ever saw the heavens
Acting so angrily?

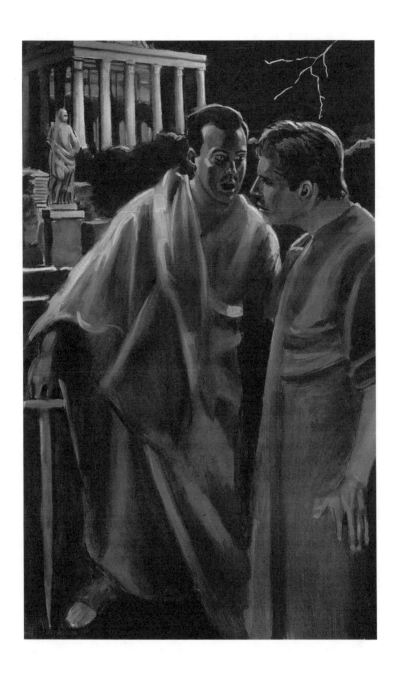

CASSIUS: Those who have known the earth
    To be full of faults. For my part,
    I have been walking in the streets tonight
    With my coat open.
    When I saw the lightning flash,
    I dared it to hit me.

CASCA: Why did you tempt the heavens?
    Men must act in fear and tremble
    When the mighty gods send such messages.

CASSIUS: You are dull, Casca. The sparks
    Of life that should be in a Roman
    Are not in you. Or else you don't use them.
    You look pale and frightened. Just think
    About what these fires, lions, and owls
    Might mean. Why are they all acting
    In such strange ways? Perhaps the heavens
    Want them to act as a warning about some
    Terrible state. I can name for you, Casca,
    A man who is most like this dreadful night.
    He thunders, storms, and roars
    As that lion did in the Capitol.
    He is a man no stronger than you or me.
    Yet he has grown as mighty and frightening
    As that lion.

CASCA: The man you mean is Caesar, isn't it?

CASSIUS: Let it be who it is.
    Woe for these times!
    Our fathers' minds are dead,
    And we are ruled with our mothers' spirits.
    Our actions show us to be womanish.

CASCA: They say that the senators
     Mean to make Caesar king tomorrow.
     He shall wear his crown by sea and land,
     In every place, except here in Italy.

CASSIUS: I know where
     I will wear this dagger then.
     No stony tower, nor prison walls,
     Nor airless dungeon, nor chains
     Can stop me. I will not be ruled
     By a tyrant such as Caesar.

(*More thunder is heard.*)

CASCA: I agree with you, Cassius.
     Every subject, with his own hand, has
     The power to overthrow the tyrants.

CASSIUS: Why is Caesar a tyrant?
     Poor man! He does not want to be a wolf,
     But he sees that the Romans are just sheep.
     He would not be a lion,
     If the Romans were not dogs.
     One who wants to make a mighty fire fast,
     Starts it with weak straws.
     What trash is Rome—to serve as the straw
     That lights so evil a thing as Caesar!
     But why am I talking like this to you?
     Perhaps you are happy to see Caesar king.

CASCA: No, Cassius.
     I feel the same as you.
     I'm with you to the end.

CASSIUS: Then we have a deal.
     Know this, Casca: I have spoken already

To some of the noblest-minded Romans.
They have agreed to support me in an act
Of honorable yet dangerous results.
They are waiting for me right now
Near the theater Pompey built.
This fearful night, the sky is like the work
We have to do—
Most bloody, fiery, and terrible.

(CINNA *enters.*)

CASCA: Quiet! Someone's coming!

CASSIUS: It's Cinna. I can tell by his walk.
He is a friend. Cinna, why are you rushing?

CINNA: To find you! Who's with you?

CASSIUS: Casca. Are the others waiting?

CINNA: Yes, they are. Oh, Cassius, if only
You could get the noble Brutus to join us!

CASSIUS: Don't worry. Good Cinna,
Take this paper. Put it on Brutus's chair
In the senate, where he will certainly see it.
Throw this one through his window.
Put another one on a public statue.
Then meet us at Pompey's theater.

CINNA: I'll be there soon.

(CINNA *exits.*)

CASSIUS: Come, Casca, you and I
Will visit Brutus before morning.
Three parts of him are ours already.
The rest of him will soon be on our side.

CASCA: The people love Brutus.
　　If he's on our side, the people will be, too.

CASSIUS: You understand very well
　　How important Brutus is to us.
　　Let us go. It is after midnight. Before day,
　　We will awake him and be sure he is ours.

(CASSIUS *and* CASCA *exit.*)

Act 2

Brutus decides that Caesar must be killed, for the good of all. He is afraid that power is dangerous and that Caesar will change after he is crowned as king. Portia, Brutus's wife, begs Brutus to tell her what is troubling him. He promises to tell her soon. After having bad dreams, Calpurnia, Caesar's wife, asks Caesar to stay home. He decides he must go to the Capitol anyway. A very nervous Portia sends a servant to the Capitol to find out what is going on there. She also asks a soothsayer for news about Caesar.

Scene 1

Brutus's garden. BRUTUS *enters.*

BRUTUS: Lucius! Come here, please!
   I wish I could sleep so soundly!
   Come on, Lucius, wake up. Awake, I say!

(LUCIUS *enters.*)

LUCIUS: You called, my lord?

BRUTUS: Light a candle in my study.
   When it is lighted, come and call me.

LUCIUS: I will, my lord. (LUCIUS *exits.*)

BRUTUS: Caesar must be stopped.
   It's for the general good. For my part,
   I have no personal reason to attack him.
   He wants to be crowned. How that might
   Change his nature is the question.
   It is the bright day that brings forth

21

The snake and demands careful walking.
Crown him? I think not!
By doing so, we would put a stinger in him.
At his will, he may do harm with it.
It is in the nature of power to be abused.
If Caesar has that much power,
There's no telling what he might do.
To speak the truth about the man,
I have always known him to be reasonable.
But it is well known that lowliness is
Young ambition's ladder.
While on that ladder,
The climber turns his face upward.
But once he gets to the top of it,
He turns his back on the ladder.
He looks in the clouds and scorns the
Lower rungs by which he did climb.
So Caesar may. We must prevent that.
He has done nothing that would
Give us an excuse not to crown him.
So we must think of him as a serpent's egg.
When hatched, it would grow dangerous.
That is why we must kill him in the shell.

(LUCIUS *enters again.*)

LUCIUS: The candle is burning, sir.
While in your study, I found this letter.
It was not there when I went to bed.

(LUCIUS *gives* BRUTUS *the letter.*)

BRUTUS: Go back to bed.
It is not yet day.
Isn't today the ides of March?

LUCIUS: I don't know, sir.

BRUTUS: Check the calendar,
     And come back to tell me.

LUCIUS: I will, sir. (LUCIUS *exits*.)

BRUTUS: The meteors whizzing in the air
     Give enough light to read by.
     (*He opens the letter and reads*.)
     "Brutus, you are sleeping! Awake!
     Rome needs you! Speak, strike!
     Brutus, you are sleeping! Awake!"

(LUCIUS *enters again*.)

LUCIUS: Sir, today is indeed March 15th.

(*Knocking within*)

BRUTUS: Thank you. Go to the gate.
     Somebody knocks. (LUCIUS *exits*.)
     Since Cassius first spoke to me
     Against Caesar, I have not slept.
     Between the thought of a dreadful thing
     And the first action of it, the time passes
     Like a fantasy or a terrible dream.
     The mind and the body seem to be
     Arguing with each other. The state of man,
     Like a little kingdom, suffers then
     What seems like a battle.

(LUCIUS *enters again*.)

LUCIUS: Sir, Cassius is at the door.
     He would like to see you.

BRUTUS: Is he alone?

LUCIUS: No, sir. There are more with him.

BRUTUS: Do you know them?

LUCIUS: No. Their hats are pulled down,
    And their faces are buried in their cloaks.

BRUTUS: Let them enter. (LUCIUS *exits*.)
    They are the plotters! They are ashamed
    To show their dangerous faces by night,
    When evils are most free. By day,
    They could not find a cave dark enough
    To hide their monstrous faces!
    They cannot hide anywhere
    Except in smiles and friendliness.

(CASSIUS, CASCA, DECIUS, CINNA, METELLUS, *and*
TREBONIUS *enter*.)

CASSIUS: Good morning, Brutus!
    Did we wake you?

BRUTUS: I have been up for a while.
    I could not sleep. Do I know these men
    Who came along with you?

CASSIUS: Yes, every one of them.
    They all respect you. Each one wishes
    You had the same opinion of yourself
    That every noble Roman has of you.

BRUTUS: They are all welcome.
    What's on your mind?

CASSIUS: May we speak in private?

(*They whisper and then return to the group.*)

BRUTUS: Give me your hands, one by one.

CASSIUS: And let us swear
    To carry out our plan.

24

BRUTUS: No, we do not need an oath!
    If our plan is good, then, countrymen,
    What need do we have to swear?
    What other bond do we need
    Than honest Romans
    Who have given their words?
    Do not stain the goodness of our plan
    Nor the strength of our spirits
    By thinking we need an oath.

CASSIUS: But what about Cicero?
    Shall we ask him?
    I think he will stand with us.

CASCA: Let us not leave him out.

CINNA: By no means.

METELLUS: Oh, let us speak to him.
    His silver hair will buy us respect,
    And make men's voices praise our deed.
    It shall be said that his judgment ruled us.
    Our youth and wildness shall seem
    To be buried in his seriousness.

BRUTUS: Let's not include him.
    He will never follow anything
    That other men begin.

CASSIUS: Then leave him out.

CASCA: Indeed, he is not fit.

DECIUS: Shall no other man be touched
    But Caesar?

CASSIUS: Good point, Decius. I think
    It is unwise to let Antony,

So well loved by Caesar, to outlive him.
He could be dangerous, too.
Let Antony and Caesar fall together.

BRUTUS: Our actions will seem too bloody.
Let's be sacrificers, not butchers.
We all stand up against the spirit of Caesar,
And in the spirit of men there is no blood.
I wish we could destroy Caesar's spirit,
Without killing the man! But, alas,
Caesar must bleed for it! Gentle friends,
Let's kill him boldly, but not in anger.
Let's carve him as a dish fit for the gods,
Not cut him up as a carcass fit for the dogs.
Antony is like an arm of Caesar's.
Once the head is gone, the arm is useless.

CASSIUS: Yet I fear him because of the
Great love he has for Caesar—

BRUTUS: Alas, good Cassius.
Do not think of him.
If he really loves Caesar,
The only harm he can do is to himself.
He might become sad and kill himself.
But that is not likely, for Antony
Enjoys his life too much. He loves sport,
And fun, and good company.

TREBONIUS: There is nothing to fear
From Antony. Do not kill him.
He will live and laugh at this later.

(*The clock strikes.*)

BRUTUS: Quiet! Listen to the clock!

CASSIUS: The clock strikes three.

TREBONIUS: It's time to part.

CASSIUS: But we don't know
If Caesar will come out today, or not.
He seems to have grown afraid
Of his own dreams, imagination,
And fantasies. He may stay away from the
Capitol because of what the seers say.

DECIUS: Never fear that. He loves to hear
That people are fooled most by those who
Play up to them. If I say that he hates
Such people, he'll agree.
In this way, I can fool him.
Let me work. I know how to get him
To come to the Capitol.

BRUTUS: By eight o'clock.
Is that a good time?

CINNA: At the latest!

CASSIUS: It's almost morning.
Friends, go home now. But remember
What you have said. Be true to your words.

BRUTUS: Good friends, look happy.
Do not let our faces show our thoughts.
Act like our Roman actors do.
Good morning to each of you.
(*All exit but* BRUTUS.)
Lucius! Are you fast asleep? No matter.

Enjoy that honey-heavy feeling.
You have no thoughts that might
Keep you from sound rest.
That is why you sleep so well.

(PORTIA, BRUTUS'S *wife, enters.*)

PORTIA: Brutus, my lord!

BRUTUS: Portia, what's going on?
Why are you awake at this hour?
It is not healthy to get up so early.

PORTIA: The same goes for you, my dear.
Last night, at supper, you got up
As if something were bothering you.
You would not tell me what it was.
And tonight, you left our bed in the middle
Of the night. Tell me, dear, what is wrong.

BRUTUS: I am not feeling well.

PORTIA: Are you sick? Is it a good idea
To walk around in the damp morning air?
No, my Brutus. I fear that you have a
Sickness in your mind.
Because I am your wife, I have a right
To know what is troubling you.
Upon my knees, I beg you,
By the vows of love and marriage,
To tell me what's bothering you.
I want to know why six or seven men
Came here tonight, hiding their faces
Even in the dark.

BRUTUS: Do not kneel, dear Portia.

PORTIA: I would not need to, dear Brutus,
    If you would only tell me what is wrong.
    Remember that I am your wife.

BRUTUS: You are my true and dear wife.
    You are as dear to me as are the tears
    That visit my sad heart.

PORTIA. If this is so, then tell the truth.
    I grant that I am a woman.
    But I am the woman you took as wife.
    And I am Cato's daughter.
    Don't you think that I am stronger
    Than most women—with such a husband
    And such a father? Tell me your problems.
    I will not tell anyone else.
    I will prove that I can be trusted.
    (*She cuts herself in the leg with a knife.*)
    If I can bear such a wound,
    Can I not bear my husband's secrets?

BRUTUS: Oh, dear God!
    Make me worthy of such a wife!
    (*Knocking within*)
    What's that? Someone is knocking!
    Portia, go inside. Later, I shall tell you
    The secrets of my heart.
    I will tell you all my plans.
    For now, please leave me quickly.
    (PORTIA *exits.*)
    Lucius, who is knocking?

(LUCIUS *enters, with* LIGARIUS.)

LUCIUS: Here is a sick man.
   He would like to speak with you.

BRUTUS: Ligarius, I've heard of you.
   Greetings.

LIGARIUS: Good morning, sir.
   I'm happy to meet you.

BRUTUS: And I'm happy to meet you.
   I wish that you were not sick!

LIGARIUS: I am not sick, sir,
   If you have any deed in mind
   That is worthy of the name of honor.

BRUTUS: I have such a deed in mind,
   Ligarius. I hope your ear is healthy
   Enough to hear about it.

LIGARIUS: By all the gods of Rome,
   I hereby throw away my sickness!
   Soul of Rome! Brave son! For you,
   I will do anything. What do you ask of me?

BRUTUS: A piece of work
   That will make sick men feel well.

LIGARIUS: But what about those well men
   Who may be made to feel sick?

BRUTUS: That may happen, too.
   I shall tell you our plan,
   As we walk along to find the man
   To whom it must be done.

LIGARIUS: Go on, then.
   With a happy heart, I will follow you.

I will do whatever you ask.
It is enough that Brutus leads me on.

(*Thunder sounds.*)

BRUTUS: Follow me, then.

(*All exit.*)

Scene 2

CAESAR'S *house. Thunder and lightning.* CAESAR *enters, in his night clothes.*

CAESAR: Neither heaven nor earth
Has been at peace tonight. Three times,
Calpurnia cried out in her sleep.
She said, "Help! They murder Caesar!"
Who's there?

(*A* SERVANT *enters.*)

SERVANT: My lord?

CAESAR: Go tell the priests to make a
Sacrifice right now.
Tell me what they think will happen.

SERVANT: I will, my lord.

(SERVANT *exits.* CALPURNIA *enters.*)

CALPURNIA: Dear husband,
I think you should stay home today.
I have never been afraid of omens before,
But now they scare me.
I have heard about terrible sights
Seen by the guards. A mother lion
Gave birth on the streets.
Graves opened, and the dead rose.

Fierce warriors were fighting in the clouds,
And ghosts screamed in the streets.
Oh, Caesar! These things seem strange,
And yes, I do fear them.

CAESAR: These omens
Are for the entire world,
As much as they are for Caesar.

CALPURNIA: When beggars die,
No comets are seen. The heavens
Blaze forth the death of princes.

CAESAR: Cowards die many times
Before their deaths.
The valiant never taste of death but once.
Of all the wonders that I have heard,
It seems to me most strange
That men should fear death.
Because it is a necessary end,
It will come when it will come.
(SERVANT *enters again.*)
What did the seers say?

SERVANT: They said that
You should not leave your house today.
Searching the body of a sacrificed animal,
They could not find a heart inside it.

CAESAR: That might only mean that
Caesar would be like an animal
Without a heart if he stayed home today.
No, I shall not stay home.
Danger knows that Caesar
Is more dangerous than he.

We are two lions born in the same litter.
I am the elder and more terrible.
Caesar shall go to the Capitol.

CALPURNIA: Alas, my lord.
Your wisdom is
Taken over by your confidence.
Do not go out today. Call it my fear—
Not your own—that keeps you at home.
Send Antony to the senate-house,
And he shall say you are not well today.
Let me, upon my knee, win in this matter.

CAESAR: To humor you, I shall stay at home.
(DECIUS *enters*.)
Here's Decius. He will tell them so.

DECIUS: Caesar, hello! Good morning!
I've come to walk you to the senate-house.

CAESAR: And you are just in time
To bring my greetings to the senators.
Tell them that I will not come today.

DECIUS: Most mighty Caesar, tell me why,
So that I won't be laughed at
When I tell them.

CALPURNIA: Say that he is sick.

CAESAR: No. I do not wish to lie to them.
Just tell them that I do not wish to come.
That is enough to satisfy them.
But for you, because you are my friend,
I will say the truth. My wife, Calpurnia,
Wants me to stay at home because

She had bad dreams last night.
She dreamed that blood poured forth
From my statue. Romans came smiling
And touched their hands to it.
She takes this as an omen, and she has
Begged me to stay at home today.

DECIUS: This dream can be seen
In a different way. When your statue
Bled, and the smiling Romans touched it,
It meant that you would bring strength
To Rome. That is what the dream meant.

CAESAR: How do you know?

DECIUS: When you hear what I have to say,
You will agree with me.
The senators have decided
To give the crown to mighty Caesar today.
If you say you will not come,
They might change their minds.

CAESAR: Calpurnia, how foolish
Your fears seem now!
I am ashamed I gave in to them.
Give me my robe, for I will go.

(BRUTUS, LIGARIUS, METELLUS, CASCA, TREBONIUS,
CINNA, *and* PUBLIUS *enter.*)

PUBLIUS: Good morning, Caesar.

CAESAR: Good morning to all of you.
What time is it?

BRUTUS: It is eight o'clock.

CAESAR: Thanks for coming so early.
(ANTONY *enters*.) Antony! Good morning!

ANTONY: The same to you, noble Caesar.

CAESAR: Trebonius, stay close to me,
So I can speak to you.

TREBONIUS: Caesar, I will. (*Aside*) I shall
Stay so close that your best friends
Will wish I had been farther away.

CAESAR: Good friends, go inside.
Drink some wine with me. Then we,
Like friends, will leave together.

BRUTUS (*aside*): It's too bad that your
So-called friends are not true.
I am sorry to think about it!

(*All exit.*)

Scene 3

A street near the Capitol. ARTEMIDORUS, *a wise
teacher, enters, reading a paper.*

ARTEMIDORUS: Caesar, beware of Brutus.
Cassius, and Casca. Watch out for Cinna.
Don't trust Trebonius. Avoid Metellus.
Decius is not your friend, nor is Ligarius. All
these men have only one thought,
And it is against Caesar.
If you fear death, look around you.
May the mighty gods defend you.

(ARTEMIDORUS *exits.*)

Scene 4

Before the house of BRUTUS. PORTIA *and* LUCIUS *enter.*

PORTIA: Lucius, run to the senate-house.

LUCIUS: Madam, what should I do?
    Run to the Capitol, and nothing else?

PORTIA: Come back with news about
    How Brutus looks. You know that
    He looked ill when he left here.
    Watch what Caesar does, and notice how
    Others act toward him. Listen!
    What noise is that?

LUCIUS: I hear nothing, madam.

PORTIA: Listen carefully. I hear a rumor,
    Like a wind, from the Capitol.

LUCIUS: Truly, madam, I hear nothing.

(SOOTHSAYER *enters.*)

PORTIA: Come here, fellow.
    Where have you been?

SOOTHSAYER: At home, good lady.

PORTIA: What time is it?

SOOTHSAYER: About nine o'clock.

PORTIA: Has Caesar gone to the Capitol?

SOOTHSAYER: Not yet.

PORTIA: Do you know if any harm
    Will come to him?

SOOTHSAYER: Not for sure, but I fear
    That much harm might come to him.

Here the street is narrow.
The mob that follows Caesar at his heels
Would crowd a weak man almost to death.
I will find an empty place, and there
I will speak to Caesar as he comes along.

(SOOTHSAYER *exits.*)

PORTIA: I must go inside. Oh, my!
How weak a thing the heart of a woman is!
I grow faint! Run, Lucius! Tell Brutus
That I am well. Come back to me again,
And tell me what he says to you.

(*All exit.*)

Act 3

Caesar goes to the Capitol, gives a speech, and is murdered. At the funeral, Brutus explains why Caesar was killed and wins the crowd over. The people are ready to name Brutus as the next leader. Then Antony speaks, changing the attitude of the crowd toward the murderers. Brutus and Cassius leave the city to escape the anger of the people. The people prepare to burn the homes belonging to the murderers.

Scene 1

Rome. In front of the Capitol. CAESAR, BRUTUS, CASSIUS, CASCA, DECIUS, METELLUS, TREBONIUS, CINNA, ANTONY, LEPIDUS, PUBLIUS, POPILIUS, ARTEMIDORUS, *and the* SOOTHSAYER *enter.*

CAESAR (*to the* SOOTHSAYER):
The ides of March have come.

SOOTHSAYER: Yes, Caesar, but have not gone.

ARTEMIDORUS: Hail, Caesar! Read this.
(*He holds out a paper.*) It is important.
It is about you and your own safety.

CAESAR: My own safety is my least worry.

ARTEMIDORUS: Do not wait, great Caesar.
Read it right now.

CAESAR: What, is the fellow mad?
Come to the Capitol.

(CAESAR *goes up to the senate-house. The rest follow.*)

POPILIUS (*to* CASSIUS): Good luck today.

CASSIUS: Luck in what, Popilius?

POPILIUS: Farewell.

(POPILIUS *moves toward* CAESAR.)

BRUTUS: What did Popilius say?

CASSIUS: He wished me good luck today.
I fear our plan is discovered.

BRUTUS: Don't worry, Cassius.
Popilius has no idea of our plan.
Look at him. He smiles, and
Caesar's face does not change.

CASSIUS: Trebonius is doing his job.
See how he gets Antony out of the way.

(ANTONY *and* TREBONIUS *exit.*)

DECIUS: Where is Metellus?

BRUTUS: Where he should be, near Caesar.

CINNA: Casca, you will strike first.

CAESAR: Are we ready to begin?
What is now wrong, that Caesar and
His senate can take steps to fix?

METELLUS: Most high, most mighty,
And most wise Caesar, I kneel here
Before you, and humbly ask—

(METELLUS *kneels.*)

CAESAR: Get up, Metellus. I know what you want.
Such a scene might change the mind of
An ordinary man. But don't be foolish enough

To think that Caesar will change his mind.
Your brother has been banished from Rome
For good reasons. If you kneel and beg
For him, I will kick you out of my way
Like a dog.

METELLUS: Is there another voice
Better than mine to speak
More sweetly in great Caesar's ear,
On my brother's behalf?

BRUTUS: Caesar, I also ask that you let
Metellus's brother return to Rome.

CAESAR: What, Brutus!

CASSIUS: Pardon him, Caesar, pardon him!
I fall as low as your foot,
To beg forgiveness for Metellus's brother.

CAESAR: If I were like you,
I could be moved. But I am not like you.
I am as constant as the northern star,
Which is unlike all other stars in the sky.
The skies are painted with many sparks.
They are all fire, and every one does shine.
But there is one that holds its place.
The world is the same. It is full of men.
The men are made of flesh and blood.
Yet of all those men, I know just one
That keeps his strong position.
He does not move. I am that one.
Let me prove it, even in this.
I banished the brother of Metellus.
My decision remains to keep him banished.

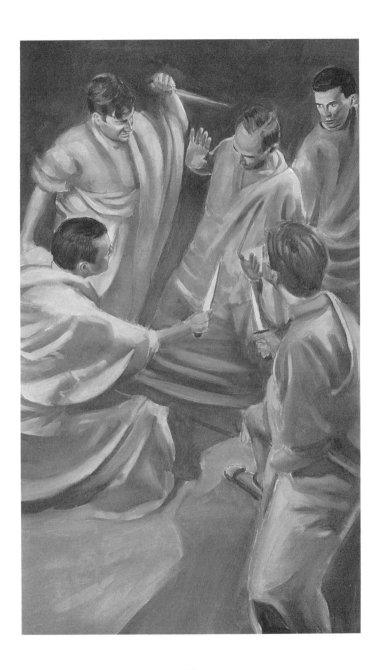

CINNA: Oh, Caesar—

CAESAR: Stop!
Would you try to lift a mountain?

DECIUS: Great Caesar—

CAESAR: I will not change my mind!

CASCA: Speak, hands, for me!

(CASCA *strikes at* CAESAR. *The other men rush toward* CAESAR, *and they stab him.*)

CAESAR: You, too, Brutus?
Then fall, Caesar! (CAESAR *dies.*)

CINNA: Liberty! Freedom!
Tyranny is dead! Run forth!
Tell the good news in the streets!

CASCA: Liberty! Freedom! At last!

BRUTUS: People and senators,
Do not be afraid. Do not run forth.
Stand still. Ambition's debt is paid.

CASCA: Tell the people, Brutus.

DECIUS: Cassius should tell them, too.

BRUTUS: Where's Publius?

CINNA: He's here, quite confused
By what he has just seen.

METELLUS: Stand close together,
In case some friend of Caesar's
Should happen to—

BRUTUS: Do not talk about that!
Publius, don't be scared.

No harm is intended toward you,
Nor to any other Roman.
Go and tell the people.

CASSIUS: Yes, leave us, Publius,
In case the people rushing at us
Might do some harm to you.

BRUTUS: Do so. Let no man pay a penalty
For this deed, but we who did it.

(TREBONIUS *enters again.*)

CASSIUS: Where is Antony?

TREBONIUS: He has fled to his house.
He is afraid and confused.
Men, women, and children stare, cry out,
And run, as if it were the end of the world.

BRUTUS: The fate of all people is the same.
Everyone must die, sooner or later.

CASSIUS: He who cuts off 20 years of life
Also cuts off 20 years of fearing death.

BRUTUS: Believe that, and we can be seen
As Caesar's friends, to have
Shortened his time of fearing death.
Stoop, Romans, stoop.
Let us bathe our hands in Caesar's blood
Up to the elbows. Let us smear our swords.
Then we will walk into the marketplace,
Waving our red weapons over our heads.
Let us all cry, "Peace, freedom, and liberty!"

CASSIUS: Stoop, then, and wash.

BRUTUS: How often will Caesar bleed
In scenes acted out in the future?
Over how many ages, from now on,
Shall this story be told
In states unborn and accents yet unknown?

CASSIUS: Every time the story is told,
We shall be called the men
That gave their country liberty.

DECIUS: Shall we go forth?

CASSIUS: Yes, every one of us.
Brutus shall lead. We will grace his heels
With the boldest and best hearts of Rome.

(A SERVANT enters.)

BRUTUS: Quiet! Someone's coming!
It's a friend of Antony's.

SERVANT: Brutus, my master sent me.
If you can promise Antony's safety,
He would like to come, to be told why
Caesar deserves to lie in death.
He said he shall not love Caesar dead
So well as Brutus living. He will follow
Brutus in his new role, with all good faith.
So says my master Antony.

BRUTUS: Your master is wise and brave.
Tell him to come. I promise he will be safe.

SERVANT: I'll tell him. (SERVANT exits.)

BRUTUS: I think Antony can be trusted.

CASSIUS: I'm not sure. I fear him greatly.

(ANTONY *enters.*)

BRUTUS: Welcome, Antony!

ANTONY (*looking down at Caesar's body*):
Oh, mighty Caesar! Do you lie so low?
Are all your conquests, glories, victories,
Reduced to this small measure? Farewell!
I do not know, gentlemen, what you plan.
Who else must die? If I must die, there's no
Better hour than Caesar's hour,
No better weapons than your swords.
They have been made rich
With the most noble blood of all this world.
I beg you, if you plan to kill me, do it now.
If I lived a thousand years, I would not find
A better time or place to die.
Here by Caesar, and by you cut off,
The choice and master spirits of this age.

BRUTUS: Antony, we will not harm you,
Though now we must seem to you bloody
And cruel. You see only our hands, and
This, the bleeding business they have done.
You do not see our hearts.
We did what we did out of pity for Rome.
For you, our swords have blunt points.
We receive you with love, good thoughts,
    and honor.

CASSIUS: Your voice shall be as strong
As any man's in the new state of Rome.

BRUTUS: Just be patient until we have calmed
The people. They are beside themselves

With fear. Soon I will tell you why I,
Who did love Caesar when I struck him,
Did what had to be done.

ANTONY: I do not doubt your wisdom.
Let each man give me his bloody hand.
I wish to shake each one. (*They all shake.*)
Gentlemen, you must think that I am
Either a coward or a flatterer.
That I did love you, Caesar, it is true.
If your spirit looks on us now,
Would this scene cause you greater pain
Than even your death? You see Antony
Shaking the bloody fingers of your foes,
In the presence of your body.
If I had as many eyes as you have wounds,
Weeping as fast as they stream forth
Your blood, that would be better than this!
Pardon me, Caesar!
Here you were cornered, brave deer!
Here you fell. And here your hunters stand.
Oh world, you were the forest to this deer,
And this, oh world, the dearest part of you.
How like a deer, struck by many hunters,
Do you lie here!

CASSIUS: Antony, I do not blame you for
Praising Caesar. But what does it mean?
Can we still count on your loyalty?

ANTONY: Of course you can!
I was merely distracted for a moment
As I looked down on Caesar.

I am friends with you all. I came to hear
Why you believe Caesar was dangerous.

BRUTUS: Our reasons were so good that
Even if you were Caesar's son,
You would be behind us.

ANTONY: That is all I came for.
That, and one more thing: I want to
Speak at his funeral, as a friend should.

BRUTUS: You shall, Antony.

CASSIUS: Brutus, a word with you.
(*Aside, to* BRUTUS) Don't be a fool.
Antony should not speak at the funeral.
Do you know how much the people
Might be moved by his words?

BRUTUS: I am not worried.
I will speak first and explain our reasons.
Before Antony speaks, I will say that
He speaks by our permission. I will say that
We wanted Caesar to have all the respect
And ceremonies he deserved.
It will work to our advantage.

CASSIUS: I do not like this idea.

BRUTUS: Antony, in your speech,
You must not blame us. Instead,
Speak all the good you can about Caesar.
Say you do it by our permission.
Otherwise, you won't speak at all.
Promise this, and you shall speak after me.

ANTONY: I shall abide by your conditions.

BRUTUS: Prepare the body, and follow us.

(*All exit but* ANTONY.)

ANTONY: Pardon me, you bleeding piece
　　Of earth, for being so meek and gentle
　　With these butchers!
　　You are the ruins of the noblest man
　　That ever lived in the tide of times.
　　Woe to the hand that shed this dear blood!
　　Over your body, I now do promise that
　　A curse shall fall upon all of Italy.
　　Caesar's spirit, looking for revenge, will
　　Cry "Havoc," and let out the dogs of war.

(*Octavius's* SERVANT *enters.*)

SERVANT: Lord Octavius is on his way.
　　He received Caesar's letter—
　　(*He sees the body.*) Oh, Caesar!

ANTONY: Go somewhere else to weep.
　　Sorrow, I see, is catching. My eyes,
　　Seeing tears in yours, begin to water.
　　Is your master coming?

SERVANT: Yes. He'll be here tomorrow.

ANTONY: Go meet him. Tell him about this.
　　Tell him Rome is not safe for him yet.
　　But before you go, help me carry the body
　　To the marketplace.

(*Both exit, with* CAESAR'S *body.*)

Scene 2

The Forum. BRUTUS *and* CASSIUS *enter, with the*
COMMONERS.

COMMONER 1: We will be satisfied! This act
   must be explained.

BRUTUS: Then follow me, and listen.
   I will tell you what has happened.

COMMONER 1: Brutus will speak. Silence!

BRUTUS: Romans, countrymen, loved ones!
   Hear me for my cause, and be silent,
   So you may hear. In the name of my honor,
   Believe what I say. If you ask why
   I rose up against Caesar, this is my answer:
   It was not that I loved Caesar less,
   But that I loved Rome more.
   Caesar would have made you all slaves.
   Wouldn't you rather be free?
   Because Caesar loved me, I weep for him.
   Because he was lucky, I was happy for him.
   Because he was brave, I honor him.
   But because he was ambitious, I killed him.
   Who here would like to be a slave?
   If any, speak; for I have offended you.
   Who here does not love his country?
   If any, speak; for I have offended you.
   I pause for a reply.

ALL: None, Brutus, none.

BRUTUS: Then none have I offended.
   (ANTONY *and others enter, with* CAESAR'S *body.*)
   Here comes his body, mourned by Antony.
   Though he had no hand in his death,
   He shall receive the benefit of it. He,
   Like all of you, shall have a place in Rome.
   I killed Caesar for the good of Rome.

I still have that dagger for myself, when
It shall please you to need my death.

ALL: Live, Brutus! Live! Live!

COMMONER 1: Have a statue made of him!

COMMONER 2: Let him be Caesar!

COMMONER 3: Caesar's better parts
Shall be crowned in Brutus.

BRUTUS: My countrymen—

COMMONER 1: Quiet! Brutus speaks.

BRUTUS: Good people, let me depart alone.
For my sake, stay here with Antony.
Honor Caesar's body by listening to his
Speech about Caesar's glories. Antony,
By our permission, will speak now.
I do beg you to listen carefully to him
While I go home. (BRUTUS *exits*.)

COMMONER 1: Let us hear Antony!

COMMONER 2: Let him speak!

ANTONY: Friends, Romans, countrymen,
Lend me your ears!
I come to bury Caesar, not to praise him.
The evil that men do lives after them.
The good is often buried with their bones.
So let it be with Caesar. The noble Brutus
Has told you that Caesar was ambitious.
If it were so, it was a serious fault,
And seriously has Caesar paid for it.
Here, thanks to Brutus and the rest—
For Brutus is an honorable man;

So are they all honorable men—
I have come to speak at Caesar's funeral.
He was my friend, faithful and just to me.
But Brutus says he was ambitious,
And Brutus is an honorable man.
Caesar brought many prisoners to Rome.
Ransom for them filled the public treasury.
Did this in Caesar seem ambitious?
When the poor cried, Caesar wept.
Ambition should be made of sterner stuff.
Yet Brutus says he was ambitious,
And Brutus is an honorable man.
You all saw that I offered Caesar the crown
Three times. Three times he refused it.
Was this ambition?
Yet Brutus says Caesar was ambitious.
And sure Brutus is an honorable man.
I speak not to disprove what Brutus said.
But I am here to speak what I do know.
You all loved Caesar once, for good cause.
What cause keeps you from crying for him now?
Oh, my! These men have lost their reason!
(ANTONY cries.) Bear with me.
My heart is in the coffin there with Caesar,
And I must pause till it comes back to me.

COMMONER 1: I think he might be right.

COMMONER 2: It seems Caesar has been greatly
    wronged.

COMMONER 3: Did you hear Antony?
    I remember that Caesar refused the crown.
    So, it is certain he was not ambitious.

COMMONER 1: Poor Antony! His eyes
  Are as red as fire from all his weeping!

COMMONER 2: No man in Rome
  Is nobler than Antony.

COMMONER 3: Quiet! He's going to speak again!

ANTONY: Yesterday, Caesar's words might
  Have stood against the world. Today,
  He lies there, and nobody shows respect.
  Countrymen, if I wanted to stir you to rage,
  I might speak against Brutus and Cassius,
  Who, you all know, are honorable men.

I will not do them wrong. I would rather
Wrong the dead, to wrong myself and you,
Before I would wrong such honorable men.
But here's a paper with the seal of Caesar.
I found it in his closet. It is his will.
If the common people heard it,
They would kiss dead Caesar's wounds and
Dip their handkerchiefs in his blood.
They would save a piece of his hair and,
Dying, mention it in their wills.
They would hand it down to their heirs.

COMMONER 4: Read the will, Antony.

ALL: The will, the will! Read Caesar's will!

ANTONY: Dear friends, I must not read it.
Know only that Caesar loved you.
You are not wood. You are not stones.
You are men. If you heard Caesar's will,
And knew how much he loved you,
What would happen then?

COMMONER 4: Read the will.
We want to hear it, Antony.

ANTONY: I should not have mentioned it.
I fear I wrong the honorable men
Whose daggers have stabbed Caesar.

COMMONER 4: They were traitors—
Not honorable men!

ALL: The will! The will!

COMMONER 2: They were murderers!
The will! Read the will!

ANTONY: Will you force me to read it?
Then make a ring around Caesar's body.
See the man who made the will.
If you have tears,
Prepare to shed them now.
You all know this robe. I remember
The first time Caesar put it on.
Look, Cassius's dagger ran through it here.
See what a tear the jealous Casca made.
This is where the beloved Brutus stabbed.
See how the blood of Caesar followed it,
As if rushing out of doors to see if
Brutus so unkindly knocked.
Brutus, as you know, was his best friend.
You know how dearly Caesar loved him!
This was the unkindest cut of all!
For when the noble Caesar saw him stab,
That is what hurt him most.
It broke his mighty heart. Holding his robe
Up to his face, great Caesar fell.
Oh, what a fall that was, my countrymen!
Then you, and I, and all of us fell down.
Bloody treason rose up over us.
Oh, now you weep. Kind souls,
Do you weep just to see his torn robe?
Look here: Here is himself, stabbed,
As you see, by traitors.

COMMONER 1: Oh, terrible sight!

COMMONER 2: Oh, noble Caesar!

COMMONER 3: Oh, day of woe!

COMMONER 4: Oh, traitors, villains!

ALL: Revenge! Find them! Burn! Kill!
Let not a single traitor live!

ANTONY: Wait, countrymen.

COMMONER 1: Listen to Antony!

COMMONER 2: We'll listen to him.
We'll follow him. We'll die with him!

ANTONY: Friends, let me not stir you up!
They who have done this are honorable.
I do not know their private reasons for this.
They will, I am sure, tell you their reasons.
I did not come, friends, to steal your hearts.
I am not a great speaker, as Brutus is.
As you know, I am a plain man.
I loved my friend, and they who knew this,
Gave me permission to speak about him.
I have neither the wit nor the talent to stir
Men's blood. I only speak as a plain man.
I tell you what you already know.
I show you sweet Caesar's wounds—
Those poor silent mouths—
And ask them to speak for me.
If I were Brutus, and Brutus were me,
Then I would have greater speaking skills.
Then I would stir up your spirits.
Then I could make Caesar's wounds speak
For themselves. They would move
The stones of Rome to rise up for revenge.

ALL: We'll have revenge!

COMMONER 1: We'll burn Brutus's house.

COMMONER 2: Let's go!

ANTONY: Wait, countrymen! Listen!

ALL: Listen to Antony! Noble Antony!

ANTONY: You are rushing off,
Without knowing why Caesar
Deserved your love! Alas, you know not!
You have forgotten the will I spoke about.

ALL: Most true. The will! Let's hear it!

ANTONY: Here it is. To every Roman,
Caesar gives 75 pieces of gold.

COMMONER 2: Oh, noble Caesar!
We'll avenge his death!

COMMONER 3: Oh, royal Caesar!

ANTONY: Listen! There's more.
He has also left you his land,
His private gardens, and his new orchards.
They are yours. You and your children
Can use them forever. Here was a Caesar!
When comes another such as he?

COMMONER 1: Never, never! Come, away!
We'll burn his body in a holy place.
Then we'll burn the traitors' houses.
Carry the body!

COMMONER 2: Start the fire!

(COMMONERS *exit, with the body. A* SERVANT *enters.*)

SERVANT: Sir, Octavius is in Rome.

ANTONY: Where is he?

SERVANT: At Caesar's house.

ANTONY: I will go there right away.

SERVANT: I heard him say that
Brutus and Cassius rode like madmen
Out through the gates of Rome.

ANTONY: They probably heard about
What the people plan to do.
Take me to Octavius.

(*Both exit.*)

Act 4

Antony, Octavius, and Lepidus plan to destroy Brutus and Cassius. They make a death list of anyone who might stand in the way of their plan. At a camp, preparing for battle against Antony's troops, Brutus and Cassius argue. After they resolve their argument, Messala arrives with news of the coming attack and of Portia's death. Brutus pretends to take the news lightly, trying to gain the admiration of Messala. That night, Brutus is visited by the Ghost of Caesar, who says he will meet Brutus at Philippi, the field of battle.

Scene 1

ANTONY'S *house in Rome.* ANTONY, OCTAVIUS, *and* LEPIDUS *enter.*

ANTONY: These many, then, shall die.
　　Their names are marked.

OCTAVIUS: Your brother must die, too.
　　Do you agree, Lepidus?

LEPIDUS: I agree.

OCTAVIUS: Mark him down, Antony.

ANTONY: He shall not live. Look,
　　With this mark I condemn him.
　　Lepidus, go to Caesar's house.
　　Get the will and bring it back here.
　　We shall decide how to cut down
　　On the costs of paying it.

LEPIDUS: Will you be waiting here?

OCTAVIUS: Here, or at the Capitol.

(LEPIDUS *exits*.)

ANTONY: He is an unimportant man,
Good for sending on errands.
Do you think he is fit to share
Power with us?

OCTAVIUS: You used to think so.
You even took his advice when we
Made up our list of who should die.

ANTONY: Octavius, I have seen more days
Than you. Even though we call Lepidus
One of us, he carries this honor
As a donkey carries bags of gold.
He groans and sweats under the load.
He is either led or driven,
As we point the way.
Soon our treasure will be where we want.
Then we will take down his load,
And turn him loose, like a donkey,
To shake his ears and graze in the pasture.

OCTAVIUS: Do as you wish,
But he is a true and brave soldier.

ANTONY: So is my horse, Octavius.
For that, I make sure he is well fed.
He is a creature that I teach to fight,
To turn, to stop, to run straight on.
His movements are directed by my spirit.
In many ways, Lepidus is just like a horse.
He must be taught and trained
And told what to do. Do not think of him

61

As anything more than a piece of property.
Now, Octavius, here is important news!
Brutus and Cassius are assembling an army.
We, too, must raise troops right away.
Let us meet with trusted friends
And discuss the present danger.
We must decide how to deal with this.

OCTAVIUS: Let us do so right away.
It is as if we are tied to the stake,
With enemies all around us.
I fear that some who smile
Have mischief in their hearts.

(*They exit.*)

Scene 2

A camp near Sardis. Outside BRUTUS'S *tent.*
BRUTUS, LUCILIUS, LUCIUS, *and the army enter.*
TITINIUS *and* PINDARUS *meet them.*

BRUTUS: Hello, Lucilius! Is Cassius near?

LUCILIUS: He's on his way.
Pindarus has come with greetings
From his master, Cassius.

PINDARUS: My master will be here soon,
Full of regard and honor.

BRUTUS: He honors me by doing so.
I look forward to seeing him, and
I hope it will be soon. (*Aside, to* LUCILIUS)
I am worried about changes in how
Cassius has been acting lately.
Have you noticed this, Lucilius?

LUCILIUS: He treats me with courtesy
  And respect, as before.
  But he does not seem as free and friendly
  As he used to be.

BRUTUS: You have described
  A close friendship cooling.
  I'm sure you've noticed, Lucilius,
  When love begins to sicken and decay,
  It also begins to seem forced.
  There are no tricks in true friendship.
  I'm beginning to wonder about Cassius.
  When do you think his army will be here?

LUCILIUS: The foot soldiers will be here
  By tonight. The cavalry has already come,
  And here is Cassius now.

(CASSIUS *and his officers enter.*)

CASSIUS: Brutus, noble friend,
  You have done me wrong.

BRUTUS: That is not true!
  Do I wrong my enemies? No!
  If not them, how could I wrong a friend?

CASSIUS: Brutus, I'm talking about—

BRUTUS: Cassius, let us speak in private.
  Before the eyes of our armies here,
  Let us not argue. They should see
  Nothing but friendship between us.
  Let us talk privately in my tent.
  Let Lucius and Titinius guard the door.

(*All exit.*)

Scene 3

BRUTUS'S *tent.* BRUTUS *and* CASSIUS *enter.*

CASSIUS: You accused one of my officers
  Of taking bribes. When I defended him,
  You failed to back me up!

BRUTUS: Let me tell you this, Cassius.
  I think you've been taking bribes yourself.
  You're well known for your itching palm!

CASSIUS: I have an itching palm?
  Are you out of your mind?
  If you were anyone else but Brutus,
  That speech would be your last!

BRUTUS: And if you were anyone else,
  You would have been punished by now!

CASSIUS: Punished!

BRUTUS: Remember the ides of March?
  Did not great Caesar bleed
  For the sake of justice?
  We who struck him were not villains,
  But honorable men. Shall we now
  Spoil our fingers with bribes?
  Shall we now sell our honor for money?
  I would rather be a dog baying at the moon
  Than to be such a Roman.

CASSIUS: Brutus, do not speak to me like that!
  I won't stand for it. You forget who I am.
  I am a soldier,
  More experienced and stronger than you.

BRUTUS: You are not, Cassius.

CASSIUS: I am.

BRUTUS: I say you are not.

CASSIUS: Say no more. I shall be forced
  To fight you.

BRUTUS: Go away, weak man!

CASSIUS: Must I stand for this?

BRUTUS: Yes, and more! From this day on,
  I'll think of you and laugh
  In mockery.

CASSIUS: Has it come to this?

BRUTUS: You say you are a better soldier.
  Let it appear so. Fight your battles well,
  And it shall please me. For myself,
  I shall be glad to hear of noble men.

CASSIUS: You wrong me, Brutus.
  I said "a more experienced" soldier,
  Not "a better one." Did I say "better?"

BRUTUS: If you did, I don't care.

CASSIUS: Do not push me.
  I may do something I will be sorry for.

BRUTUS: You have already done
  Something you should be sorry for.
  I am not afraid of your threats, Cassius.
  I am armed so strongly in honesty
  That your threats pass me by like the wind.
  I asked you for certain sums of gold,
  Which you have denied me.
  I cannot raise money by evil means.
  By heaven, I would rather sell my blood

For coins than take bribes from peasants!
I asked you for gold to pay my soldiers,
And you have denied me.
Would I have done the same to you?
If Brutus ever treated a friend like that,
Get ready, gods! Use your thunderbolts,
And dash him to pieces!

CASSIUS: I did not deny you the money.

BRUTUS: You did.

CASSIUS: I did not. It was just some fool
Who told you that. You break my heart.
A friend should bear his friend's burdens.
But you make mine greater than they are.

BRUTUS: This is not true.

CASSIUS: You no longer care for me.

BRUTUS: I do not care for your faults.

CASSIUS: A friend could never see them.

BRUTUS: A flatterer would not see them,
Though they are as big as mountains.

CASSIUS: Cassius is weary of this world!
Hated by a friend he loves,
All his faults seen and memorized.
Oh, I could weep my spirit from my eyes!
There is my dagger, and here is my heart.
If you are a Roman, take it out.
I, who denied you gold, give my heart.
Strike as you did at Caesar. I know
That even when you hated him the most,
You loved him more
Than you ever loved Cassius.

BRUTUS: Put your dagger away.
Calm down. Perhaps I was wrong.

CASSIUS: Give me your hand.
Let us shake on our friendship.

BRUTUS: Indeed we shall.
I am sorry I ever doubted our friendship.

(A POET, LUCILIUS, TITINIUS, *and* LUCIUS *enter. They stand outside Brutus's tent.*)

POET: Let me go in to see the generals.
There is some argument between them.
They should not be left alone.

LUCILIUS: You may not enter now.

CASSIUS: What's the matter out there?

POET: For shame, generals!
Two men like you should make amends.
For haven't you always been good friends?

CASSIUS: Ha, ha! What a bad poet he is!

BRUTUS: Go away, you old fool!
Get out of here!

(POET *exits.*)

BRUTUS: Lucilius and Titinius,
Tell the commanders to prepare
Their troops for the night.

CASSIUS: Then come back here,
And bring Messala with you.

(LUCILIUS *and* TITINIUS *exit.*)

BRUTUS: Lucius, a jug of wine!

(LUCIUS *exits.*)

CASSIUS: I've never seen you so angry.

BRUTUS: Oh, Cassius, I am sick
    With many sorrows. Portia is dead.

CASSIUS: What? Portia?

BRUTUS: She is dead.

CASSIUS: Oh, what a terrible loss!
    How did she die?

BRUTUS: She was worried about me.
    Then she heard that Antony and Octavius
    Were getting armies together to fight
        against us.
    This made her even more worried.
    When her servants were out,
    She swallowed burning coals.

CASSIUS: And died from that?

BRUTUS: Yes.

CASSIUS: Oh, that is awful!

(LUCIUS *enters again, with wine and candles.*)

BRUTUS: Speak no more of her.
    Give me a cup of wine.
    In this I bury all unkindness, Cassius.

(*He drinks.*)

CASSIUS: My heart is thirsty
    For those noble words.
    Fill, Lucius, till the wine overflows the cup.
    I cannot drink too much of Brutus's
        friendship.

(*He drinks.* TITINIUS *enters again, with* MESSALA.)

BRUTUS: Come in, Titinius!
(LUCIUS *exits*.) Welcome, Messala!
We need to talk. Sit by the candlelight.
Messala, I have received letters
That Antony and Octavius are leading
Armies against us. They are near Philippi.

MESSALA: I have received letters
That say the same thing.

BRUTUS: What else have you heard?

MESSALA: Through certain lawful means,
Antony, Octavius, and Lepidus
Have put to death 100 senators.

BRUTUS: Our letters do not agree.
I heard that only 70 senators have died.
Cicero was one.

CASSIUS: Cicero?

BRUTUS: Yes. Cicero is dead.

MESSALA: In the letters you received,
Were there any from your wife?

BRUTUS: No.

MESSALA: Did anybody write to you about her?

BRUTUS: No, Messala.

MESSALA: I think that is strange.

BRUTUS: Why do you ask?
Did you hear anything about her?

MESSALA: No, my lord.

BRUTUS: Now, as you are a Roman,
Tell me the truth.

MESSALA: Then, as you are a Roman,
    Hear the truth I tell:
    She is dead, and by a strange manner.

BRUTUS: Well, farewell, Portia.
    We all must die, Messala.
    In knowing that she must die sometime,
    I am able to accept the news now.

MESSALA: Even great men must accept
    great losses.

CASSIUS: I know as much about philosophy
    As anyone else. Even so, if it were my wife,
    I don't think I could bear it.

BRUTUS: Well, we must get on with
    The work of life. What do you think
    Of marching to Philippi right away?

CASSIUS: I do not think it's a good idea.

BRUTUS: Why?

CASSIUS: I think it would be better
    To let the enemy come after us.
    That way, their soldiers will be tired.
    We can stay here, rest, and prepare for
        battle.

BRUTUS: Good reasons must give way
    To better ones. The people who live
    Between Philippi and here are not loyal
    To us. They will join the enemies' armies.
    It would be better if we went to Philippi
    And had those people at our back.

CASSIUS: Listen, Brutus—

BRUTUS: No, you listen, Cassius.
There is a tide in the affairs of men.
If it is taken at the flood,
It leads on to fortune.
If not, all the voyages of their lives
Are bound in shallows and in miseries.
We are now floating on such a full sea.
We must take the current now,
Or lose everything.

CASSIUS: Then you go ahead.
We'll follow and meet them at Philippi.

BRUTUS: The deep of night has come.
We will rest first and leave early.
Is there any more to say?

CASSIUS: No more. Good night.
Early tomorrow we will rise and leave.

BRUTUS: Good night, noble Cassius.
Sleep well.

CASSIUS: Oh, my dear friend!
This evening had a bad beginning.
Let nothing come between us again!

BRUTUS: Good night, dear friend.

(CASSIUS *exits.* BRUTUS *reads, by the light of a candle. The* GHOST OF CAESAR *enters.*)

BRUTUS: What is wrong with this candle?
It is not burning well! Oh! Who is here?
I think something is wrong with my eyes.
What are you? Are you anything?

Are you a god, an angel, or a devil
That has come to make my blood cold?
Tell me what you are!

GHOST: Your evil spirit, Brutus.

BRUTUS: Why have you come?

GHOST: To tell you this:
I shall see you at Philippi.

BRUTUS: Well, then we shall meet again.

GHOST: Yes. At Philippi.

BRUTUS: I will see you there, then.
(GHOST *exits.*)
Evil spirit, were you really here?
I will ask the guard. Guard!
Come here!

(GUARD *enters.*)

GUARD: Yes, my lord?

BRUTUS: Did you see anyone?

GUARD: No, my lord.

BRUTUS: Go and tell Cassius
To start out for Philippi at once.
We will follow him.

GUARD: It shall be done, my lord.

(BRUTUS *and* GUARD *exit.*)

Act 5

*Returning from battle against Octavius,
Cassius sees more troops approaching. Wrongly
believing they are enemy troops, he loses all
hope for victory and asks Pindarus to kill him.
When Titinius discovers Cassius's dead body, he
kills himself. Lucilius, pretending to be Brutus,
is captured by Antony's troops. Antony sends his
soldiers to search for Brutus. When Brutus sees
that the battle is lost, he runs upon his own
sword. Antony calls Brutus the "noblest Roman
of them all."*

Scene 1

The plains of Philippi. OCTAVIUS, ANTONY, *and
their army enter.*

OCTAVIUS: Now, Antony,
　　Our hopes are answered.
　　You said the enemy would not come down,
　　But would keep to the hills.
　　You were wrong. They will meet us here.
　　They are on their way to Philippi right now.

ANTONY: I know why they are doing this.
　　They are pretending to be brave,
　　Thinking it will scare us. But it won't.

(*A* MESSENGER *enters.*)

MESSENGER: Get ready, generals.
　　The enemy comes on bravely.
　　Their battle flags are out.

ANTONY: Octavius, lead your men
  To the left side of the field.
  I'll take the right.

(BRUTUS, CASSIUS, *and their army enter, followed by* LUCILIUS, TITINIUS, MESSALA, *and others.*)

BRUTUS: We have come to talk.

ANTONY: That is fine with us.

OCTAVIUS (*to his men*): Do not move
  Until you see the signal.

BRUTUS: Words before the fighting,
  Is that it, countrymen?

OCTAVIUS: Not that we love words better,
  As you do.

BRUTUS: Good words are better than
  Bad strikes, Octavius.

ANTONY: In your bad strikes, Brutus,
  You give good words.
  Remember the hole you made
  In Caesar's heart, as you cried,
  "Long live! Hail, Caesar!"

CASSIUS: Antony, we still do not know
  About the strength of your strikes.
  As for your words, they rob the bees
  And leave them without honey.

ANTONY: Without their stingers, too?

BRUTUS: Oh, yes, and without sound.
  For you have stopped their buzzing, too.
  You very wisely threaten before you sting.

ANTONY: Villains! You gave no warning
     When your daggers hacked one another
     In the sides of Caesar.
     You showed your teeth like apes,
     And bowed like servants,
     Kissing Caesar's feet. Then Casca,
     Like a dog, struck Caesar on the neck.

CASSIUS: Now, Brutus, if you had
     Listened to me and attacked them,
     You would not have to hear such words!

OCTAVIUS: I draw my sword on traitors!
     I will not put it away again until
     Caesar's 33 wounds are avenged—
     Or until I fall in battle!

BRUTUS: There are no traitors here,
     Unless they came with you!

OCTAVIUS: I wish you were right.
     I was not born to die on Brutus's sword.

BRUTUS: Young man, you could not
     Wish for a more noble death!

OCTAVIUS: Come, Antony, let's go!
     Traitors, if you dare to fight today,
     Come to the field. If not today,
     Come when you find the courage.

(ANTONY, OCTAVIUS, *and the army exit.*)

CASSIUS: Messala, today is my birthday,
     And the signs are not good.
     Ravens and crows fly over our heads,

Looking at us as if we were sickly prey.
This is a bad day to fight.

MESSALA: Do not believe that!

CASSIUS: I only half-believe it.
I am strong in spirit and determined
To meet any danger head-on.
Now, Brutus, since the future
Is not certain, let's imagine the worst
That could happen. If we lose this battle,
What will you do? Will you be led through
The streets of Rome as a captive?

BRUTUS: No, Cassius, no!
Brutus will never go in chains to Rome.
The work begun on the ides of March
Must be finished today.
Whether we meet again, I do not know.
Therefore, let us say good-bye now.
Forever and forever, farewell, Cassius!
If we do meet again, we shall smile.
If not, then this parting was well made.

CASSIUS: Farewell, Brutus!
If we do meet again, we'll smile indeed.
If not, it's true this parting was well made.

BRUTUS: Why, then, lead on.
Oh, if only I could know the end
Of this day's business before it is over!
But it is enough that when the day is done,
The end will be known. Come, let's go!

(*All exit.*)

Scene 2

The battlefield. BRUTUS *and* MESSALA *enter.*

BRUTUS: Ride, Messala. Ride!
    I see a weakness in Octavius's army.
    Tell Cassius to attack him right away!

(*Both exit.*)

Scene 3

Another part of the field. CASSIUS *and* TITINIUS
enter.

CASSIUS: Oh, look, Titinius!
    I have turned enemy to my own men.
    This flag-bearer was turning back.
    I killed the coward. Then I took the flag.

TITINIUS: Oh, Cassius,
    Brutus told us to attack too early.
    We are surrounded by Antony's men!

(PINDARUS *enters.*)

PINDARUS: Go back, sir! Get away!
    Antony has captured your tents!
    You'd better retreat!

CASSIUS: This hill is far enough away.
    Look, Titinius. Are those my tents
    That are burning over there?

TITINIUS: They are, my lord.

CASSIUS: Titinius, quick! Ride over there!
    See if those troops are friends or enemies.

TITINIUS: Right away, sir! (*He exits.*)

CASSIUS: Pindarus, go higher on that hill.
Watch Titinius. Tell me what happens.
(PINDARUS *climbs the hill.*)
Today is my birthday.
Time has come around, full circle.
On the day I began, that day shall I end.
My life has run its course.
(*to* PINDARUS) What do you see up there?

PINDARUS (*shouting*): Oh, my lord!
Titinius is surrounded by men on horses.
They are shouting with joy.
It looks as if they have captured him!

CASSIUS: Come down, look no more.
Oh, coward that I am, to live so long,
To see my best friend taken before my eyes!
(PINDARUS *comes down from the hill.*)
Come here, Pindarus. Remember the day
I took you prisoner in battle? On that day,
You promised to do whatever I asked you
In return for your life. Come now.
Keep your promise,
And you will be free once again.
Take this sword that ran through Caesar,
And run it through my chest.
When my face is covered, as it is now,
Guide the sword.
(PINDARUS *stabs* CASSIUS *with the sword.*)
Caesar, you are avenged
By the sword that killed you. (*He dies.*)

PINDARUS: So, I am free. I would rather
Not have my freedom in such a way.

Oh, Cassius, I shall run far from here,
Where no Roman shall ever find me.

(PINDARUS *exits.* TITINIUS, *who had not been captured after all, enters again, with* MESSALA.)

MESSALA: So far, neither side is winning.
Cassius's troops were beaten by Antony.
But Brutus won out over Octavius.

TITINIUS: This news will comfort Cassius.

MESSALA: Where did you leave him?

TITINIUS: On this hill with Pindarus.

MESSALA: Is that Cassius,
Lying on the ground over there?

TITINIUS: I'm afraid it is! He's dead!
Oh, setting sun, as you sink tonight
In your red rays, so in his red blood
Has Cassius's day set.
The sun of Rome is set! Our day is gone.
Cassius must have thought we had lost!

MESSALA: Oh, what a terrible mistake!

TITINIUS: I wonder where Pindarus is.

MESSALA: Find him, Titinius, while I go
To meet the noble Brutus. I will tell him
What happened to Cassius.

TITINIUS: Hurry, then, Messala,
And I will look for Pindarus.
(MESSALA *exits.*)
Why did you send me forth, brave Cassius?
Couldn't you tell that I had met friends?
They put this crown of victory on my head,

And told me to give it to you!
Did you not hear their shouts of joy?
You must have misunderstood everything.
But, here, put this crown on your head.
Brutus told me to give it to you, and I shall.
And come, Cassius's sword.
Find Titinius's heart. (*He kills himself.*)

(MESSALA *enters again, with* BRUTUS, *young* CATO, *and others.*)

BRUTUS: Where is Cassius's body?

MESSALA: Over there.
Titinius is mourning it.

BRUTUS: Titinius's face is upward.

CATO: Oh, no! He is dead, as well!

BRUTUS: Oh, Caesar, you are still mighty!
Your spirit walks about,
And turns our swords on us.

CATO: Look at this!
Brave Titinius has crowned the dead
Cassius!

BRUTUS: Are there any two Romans living
Such as these two?
The last of all the Romans, farewell!
It is impossible that Rome will ever see
Any others as good as you.
I owe more tears than I can ever shed.
I shall find time, Cassius. I shall find time.
Come, friends, send his body home
For the funeral. Come, young Cato,
Let us go to the battlefield.

It is three o'clock. Romans, before night
We shall try to win in a second fight.

(*All exit.*)

Scene 4

Another part of the field. BRUTUS, MESSALA, *young* CATO, LUCILIUS, *and* FLAVIUS *enter.*

BRUTUS: Countrymen, hold up your heads!

(BRUTUS *exits.*)

CATO: Of course we shall!
Who will go with me?
I will announce my name on the field.
I am Cato, enemy of tyrants,
My country's friend, I am Cato!

(SOLDIERS *enter and fight.*)

LUCILIUS: And I am Brutus!
(*Young* CATO *falls.*)
Oh, young and noble Cato, are you down?
Why, you died as bravely as Titinius!

SOLDIER 1 (*to* LUCILIUS): Give up, or die!

LUCILIUS: I would rather die than give up!
Kill me, and you kill Brutus.
Be honored in his death.

SOLDIER 1: We'd better not kill Brutus!
We'll take him prisoner.

(ANTONY *enters.*)

SOLDIER 2: Antony, Brutus is our prisoner.

ANTONY (*looking around*): Where is he?
He is not here.

LUCILIUS: He is safe, Antony.
　　I promise you that no enemy
　　Shall ever take the noble Brutus alive.
　　The gods will defend him from such shame!

ANTONY (*to* SOLDIER 2): This man
　　Was simply posing as Brutus
　　To protect him. But he is still a prize.
　　Keep him safe. Treat him kindly.
　　I would rather have such men as friends
　　Than as enemies. Go on now,
　　And see whether Brutus is alive or dead.
　　Then come to Octavius's tent,
　　And tell me what you have found out.

(*All exit.*)

Scene 5

Another part of the field. BRUTUS *and* STRATO *enter.*

BRUTUS: Come, friend. Rest on this rock.
　　It looks as if we cannot win this fight.
　　Last night, Caesar's ghost appeared to me.
　　I know my last hour has come.

STRATO: Not so, my lord.

BRUTUS: No, I am sure it has, Strato.
　　You see how the fighting is going.
　　Our enemies have beaten us.
　　I will not be taken alive. Good friend,
　　We have known each other for a long time.
　　In the name of our long friendship,
　　I ask you to hold my sword,
　　While I run on it.

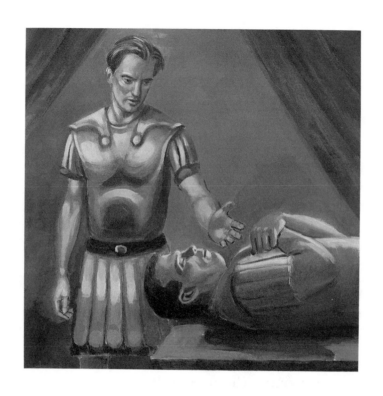

STRATO: Give me your hand first.
  Farewell, my lord.

BRUTUS: Farewell, good Strato.
  (*He charges into his sword.*)
  Caesar, now you are avenged.

(BRUTUS *dies.* OCTAVIUS, ANTONY, MESSALA, LUCILIUS,
and the army enter.)

MESSALA: Strato, where is Brutus?

STRATO: He is free from this life, Messala.
  Brutus killed himself,
  And no other man can have that honor.

MESSALA: How did he die, Strato?

STRATO: I held the sword, and he ran on it.

ANTONY (*looking at* BRUTUS'S *body*):
    This was the noblest Roman of them all.
    All the others did what they did
    Out of envy for great Caesar.
    Brutus alone acted because he thought
    It was for the good of Rome.
    His life was gentle, and his qualities
    So good that Nature might stand up
    And say to all the world, "This was a man!"

OCTAVIUS: Because he was so good,
    Let us give him the respect he deserves.
    Let his body lie in my tent tonight.
    He will have a proper burial later.
    Call the soldiers to rest, and we'll go away,
    To share the glories of this happy day.

(*All exit.*)